This Book has happened because of you!

I dedicate this book to my mother who instilled in me, knowledge and therefore a true understanding of my wonderful faith but more so for her love and her belief of me becoming an author/illustrator and writing once again! You are the inspiration that excites me to create.

To my father who I know admires all which I put my hand and mind to achieving, juggling myriad things that each day in my busy world demands! You are the force that moves my fingers into action!

Thank you both for your love.

To my two little "princesses" who will always be part of my continuing story.

And last but never least, to my doggy friend Rosa, I apologise for the few missed walkies while I was engrossed in writing this book.

Published by Ava Mehta
Content Copyright © AVA MEHTA 2016
Illustrations Copyright © AVA MEHTA 2016
All rights reserved
ISBN 978-0-9955121-0-8

Further copies of this book m: ... :hefirstnavjote@hotmail.com

Introduction

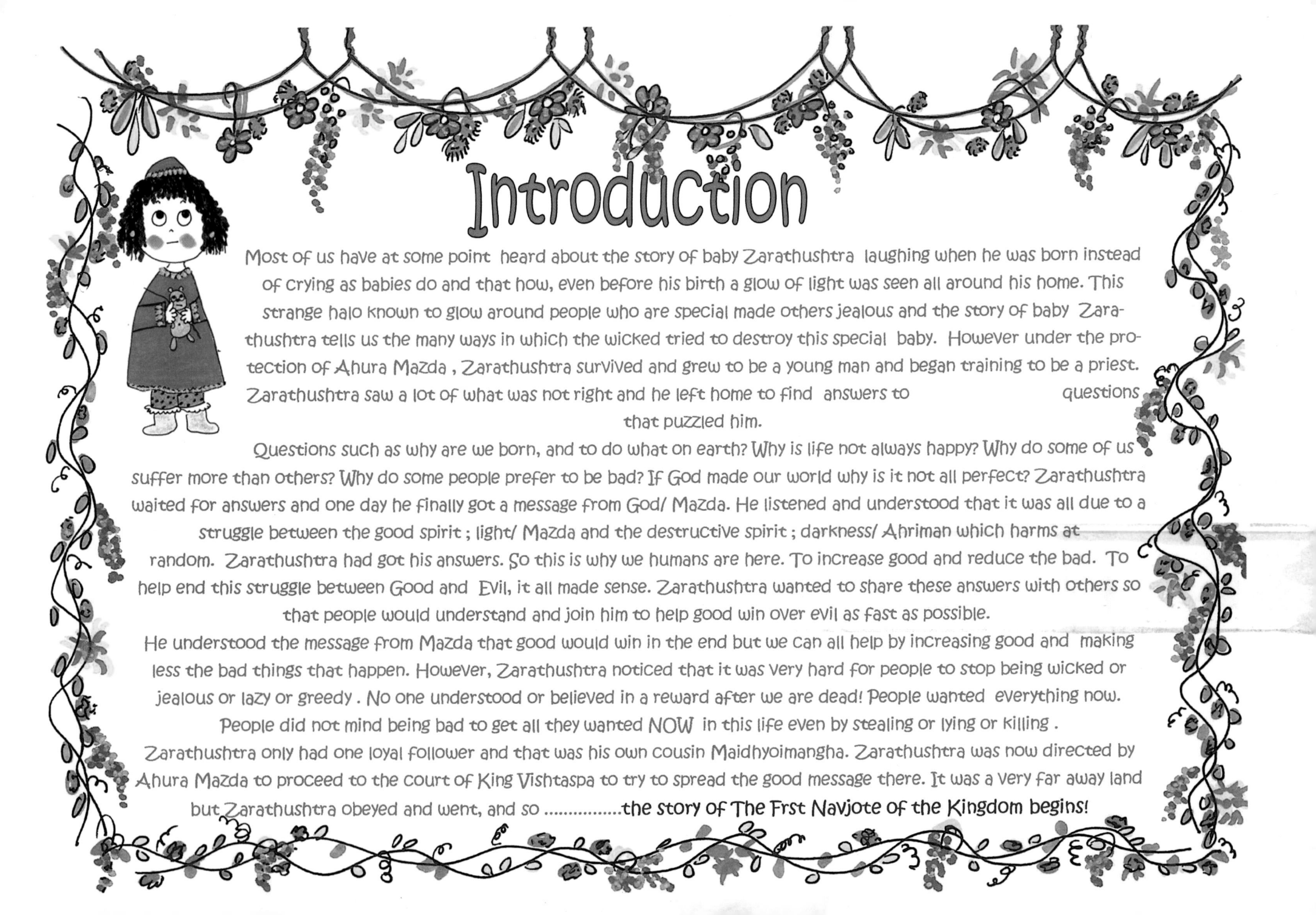

Most of us have at some point heard about the story of baby Zarathushtra laughing when he was born instead of crying as babies do and that how, even before his birth a glow of light was seen all around his home. This strange halo known to glow around people who are special made others jealous and the story of baby Zarathushtra tells us the many ways in which the wicked tried to destroy this special baby. However under the protection of Ahura Mazda, Zarathushtra survived and grew to be a young man and began training to be a priest. Zarathushtra saw a lot of what was not right and he left home to find answers to questions that puzzled him.

Questions such as why are we born, and to do what on earth? Why is life not always happy? Why do some of us suffer more than others? Why do some people prefer to be bad? If God made our world why is it not all perfect? Zarathushtra waited for answers and one day he finally got a message from God/ Mazda. He listened and understood that it was all due to a struggle between the good spirit ; light/ Mazda and the destructive spirit ; darkness/ Ahriman which harms at random. Zarathushtra had got his answers. So this is why we humans are here. To increase good and reduce the bad. To help end this struggle between Good and Evil, it all made sense. Zarathushtra wanted to share these answers with others so that people would understand and join him to help good win over evil as fast as possible.

He understood the message from Mazda that good would win in the end but we can all help by increasing good and making less the bad things that happen. However, Zarathushtra noticed that it was very hard for people to stop being wicked or jealous or lazy or greedy . No one understood or believed in a reward after we are dead! People wanted everything now. People did not mind being bad to get all they wanted NOW in this life even by stealing or lying or killing .

Zarathushtra only had one loyal follower and that was his own cousin Maidhyoimangha. Zarathushtra was now directed by Ahura Mazda to proceed to the court of King Vishtaspa to try to spread the good message there. It was a very far away land but Zarathushtra obeyed and went, and so ....the story of The Frst Navjote of the Kingdom begins!

The story of **The First Navjote** is about two little princesses who are the fictional daughters of King Vishtaspa and Queen Hutaosa and their encounter and fascination with their strange visitor Zarathushtra. One fine day Zarathushtra finally arrives at the court of the King and Queen. The rest is within the story of ' THE FIRST NAVJOTE.'

It is my hope, that through the narrative of The First Navjote, children can be guided and shown that we all have responsibility however small to make the world a **happier** and **better** place to live in whatever the situation we may find ourselves in. In the book I have given a very simple explanation of the sacred thread, (Kushti) ritual and the five Kushti prayers. I have explained **why** we recite these prayers through the princesses way of thinking and reasoning which children will be better able to identify with. The names of each prayer are also embedded into the story itself so that the reader can relate the prayer to a given circumstance in the tale as it progresses.

All drawings, colouring and the written matter throughout the story are created and hand done by Ava.

I have endeavoured to highlight the Power of Prayer and to show children how their Good thoughts, Words and Actions however small hastens the winning of Good over Evil which is the purpose of life as explained by Zarathushtra.

I hope that both children and adults enjoy this book as they absorb facts and that they 'devour' all that each illustrated character represents without realising how much learning is taking place as they read and laugh together.

Ava Mehta

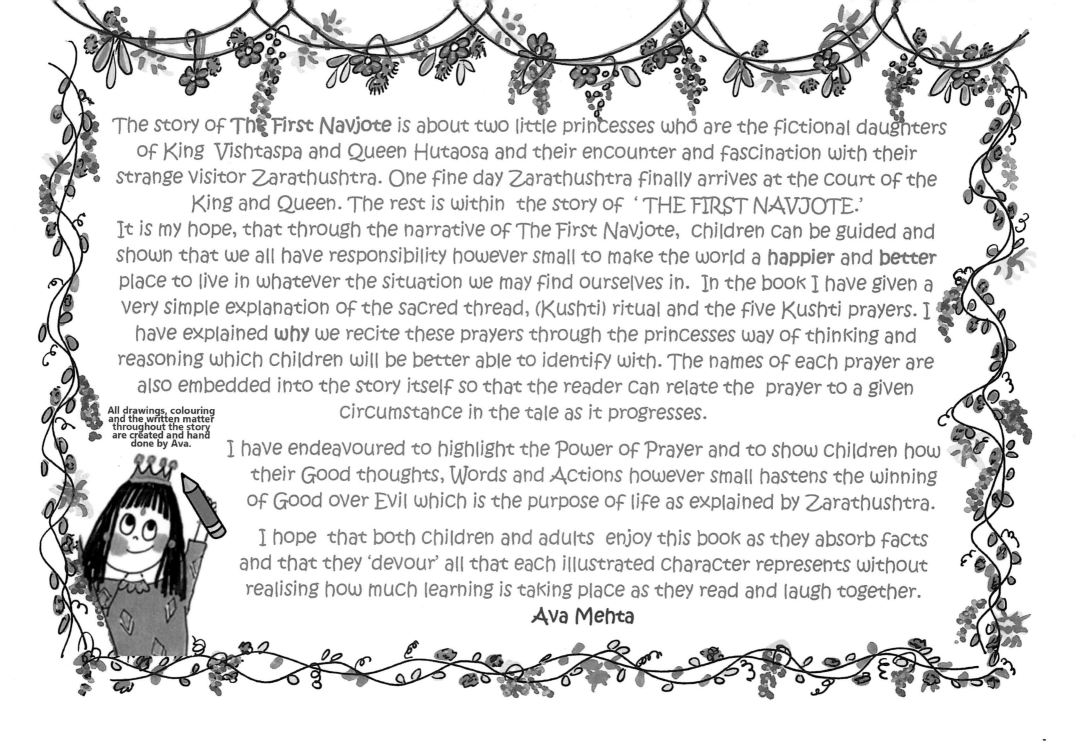

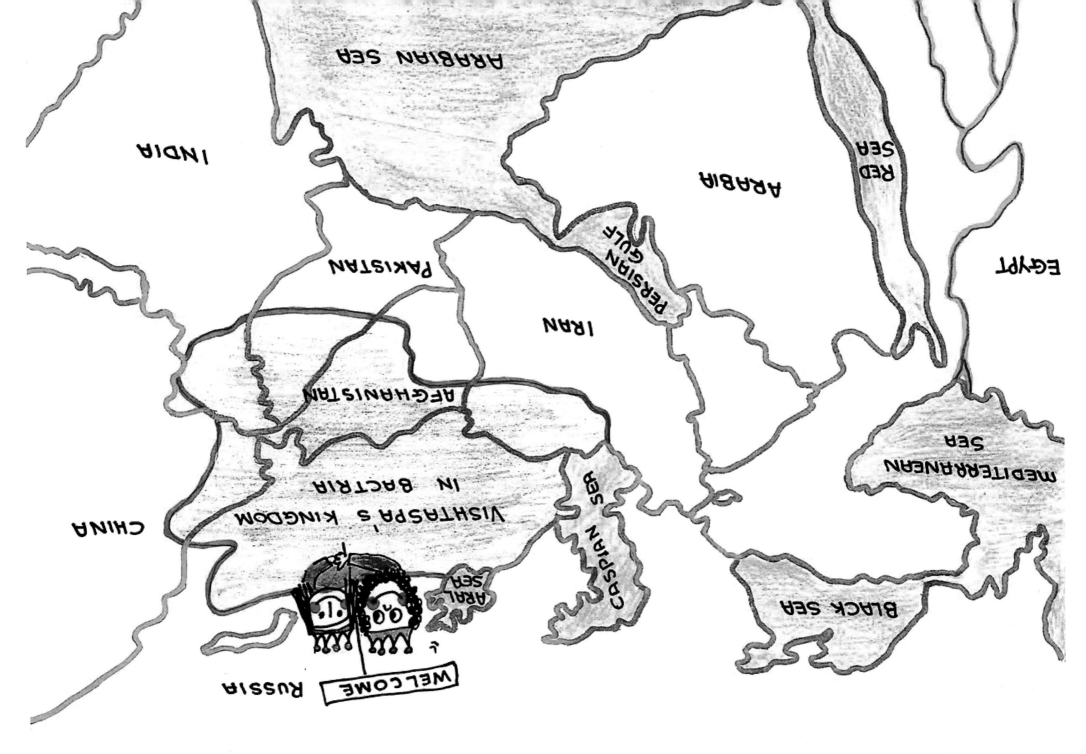

Both princesses ran to their bedroom to not lose sight of the shining light

"you're name means star, princess Tishtrya but this is certainly a man on a camel and the light is a lantern he is carrying."

"I shall still say I see a golden star on the road."

Both the princesses were right!

Because when the man dismounted and strode towards them, they saw that indeed it was a man with a lantern, but also a man with GOLDEN RAYS streaming out of his turbaned head.

"there you go again Tishtrya!
What's on his head is a crown.
Just a crown, nothing more, nothing less."

"sigh! why does my sister have such a wild imagination!"

"look carefully. It's a star.
A shiny star on his head, like I said before!

Hello Mr. You are so radiant."

Being princesses, they had seen and touched and even played with the exquisite crowns and tiaras which their parents wore on state occasions.

Not one to be put down easily Tishtrya started to argue.

"I'm puzzled. Crowns are made of solid gold and silver. His is not! His is a band of light. It's glowing around his head. Must be a glow crown?"

°°definately not a crown so he's no king!

Before the argument could develop into a quarrel, the man gently asked:

"Is this the way to enter the palace of King Vishtaspa?"

"Tishtrya.... stop it. You are meant to be a princess!"

"Yes it is". They replied in unison. "Our father is the king."

"Are you a magician?" enquired Tishtrya.

"She asks you that because of your shining crown". explained Jehanara, pointing to the sparkling halo.

"Shall we tell our father, the king that you wish to see him?"

??

"But what's your name? What do you do?"

With a reassuring smile the stranger answered the children saying,

"I am not a magician but I would like to meet the king.

My name is Zarathushtra Spitama.

I have a message for your father from Ahura Mazda."

a real angel!!
WOW.

Before Tishtrya could put her perplexing thoughts into words, Jehanara spoke out.

" like our father and mother, the king and queen of this land, Tishtrya and I like visitors who come from far away places. They have so much to tell us. So many stories.

"yes please, wait here, angel."
"sigh!"
wish I had my autograph book!"

But lately we've had some bad people entering the palace and stealing things and so we have to be careful who we allow in, you see.
Please wait here".

The princesses ran to their parents who told them to bring the kind man in.

While the royal couple stayed up all night to listen to Zarathushtra tell them about Ahura Mazda (the Great God who is also known as Hormuzd) who was totally Good, not everyone was happy with what the stranger had to say.

Zarathushtra soon realised that here too, the priests had power over the people's thinking.

They scoffed at the demonstration Zarathushtra made with his belt, the kushti, with the words of the Ahura Mazda Khodae prayer.

" How is it possible to whip away what you call evil forces with words, words and more words?

As for the two loops you made with a bridge between to symbolise two worlds, what two worlds are you talking about ?

" and that string sure looks like a cowboy lasso ! "

" hey, cowboy preacher. "

STOP WORRYING, MR. WORRIERJEE !! REMEMBER HE ALSO PREACHED THAT HIS MAZDA DOESN'T PUNISH. STOP WORRYING.

But what if he's right and we make a BAD CHOICE. He's warning us about the consequences !

" he's tying himself in knots !! "

" he's crazy! close your ears and eyes and mind. "

'ouch'

YEAH! START LOOTING !! NOT LOSING.

" hey, you are loopy, like the two loops you made in your funny string. "

" hee hee.

" ha ha

" LOOT AWAY! "

'dad, I'm getting badly influenced

YEAH! ONE LIFE TO GET RICH.

"PAPA WHICH WORLD IS HE

Zarathushtra further explained,
Those who have done GOOD on earth
will feel the bridge to be WIDE and EASY to cross(when they return
to the light – heaven.)
They will skip happily back into the spirit world.

LA DEE LA DEE DA !!

"see you good persons at the end of time !!"

"when's the end of time?"

"the journey is so smooth."

"WHY did I cheat WHY did I lie WHY WHY WHY?"
"I'm already regretting all my earthly bad doings."

"I'm dead but I can't walk the line. I'm so scared!"

"like on a first class flight."

"I made so sure of doing my good thoughts, good words and good deeds on earth."

"worse than a moving trapeze."

"will prayers work now !! how long must I regret all my badness done on earth?"

"that's my aim !! will a bribe work to get there easily?

SPIRIT WORLD

"Thats me there! This philosophy gives me regrets already!!

HELP

STOLEN

EARTH

"I think I'm dropping down into darkness and regret." Now I have to suffer till the end of time."

FAN OF BAD STUFF
lie hate kill kick steal

?

If people have NOT done enough of good, they find the bridge too narrow and hard to cross. These people are now frightened and think they are falling and they enter a dark place they have made for themselves. (hell).
ONLY AFTER SUFFERING AT THE END OF TIME (AFTER A LOT OF REGRETTING) WILL THEY JOIN THE good people.

Everything comes from a spirit world and then enters into bodies in the physical world to work for Ahura Mazda.

'what, oh what are we going to do? Our king and Queen are in awe!'

"he's teaching them cat's cradle."

"I'm learning that knot in boy scouts!"

'are women allowed your kushti too.'

'sire, do you have the time? You have other commitments too.'

"oops! loop loop pull of the bridge got me all tied up!"

"skipping ropes don't do the trick!"

'I like all you say. May I try to make the two loops to represent the two worlds with a bridge connecting them.'

"its like daddy wants to play k'nex or lego!"

"He wants to be little and play knotting games."

The gathering dispersed, but the murmuring in the palace continued. Some said the king and queen had fallen under the spell of the self-appointed Merchant of Good, who had found his way to Bactria, from the land of Aryana Vaeja where he had failed to establish his new ideas.

POISON

KILL

FEAR

DEATH

DESTROY

BLOOD

LETS HATCH AN EVIL PLOT. ITS OUR ONLY WAY TO BE SAVED.

"we have to be clever. killing Zarathushtra will make us BAD in our king's eyes. we have to plan something different."

"we'll just have to kill the man, after all his goody God won't call for him."

"Our king and Queen are in a trance because of that Zarathushtra chap."

"I wish I could do a magic trance so the king adores me!"

"what can we possibly do?"

"If his God doesn't kill, how do his people die? Do we poison them all? I don't get it!"

"I can do black magic on you!"

"I think I'm already in love with you."

"I could frighten him away with my scary faces."

"my concoction is completely deadly. Try some anyone?"

anything for m...

They'll... are who Super! now these frie...

LURE LURE

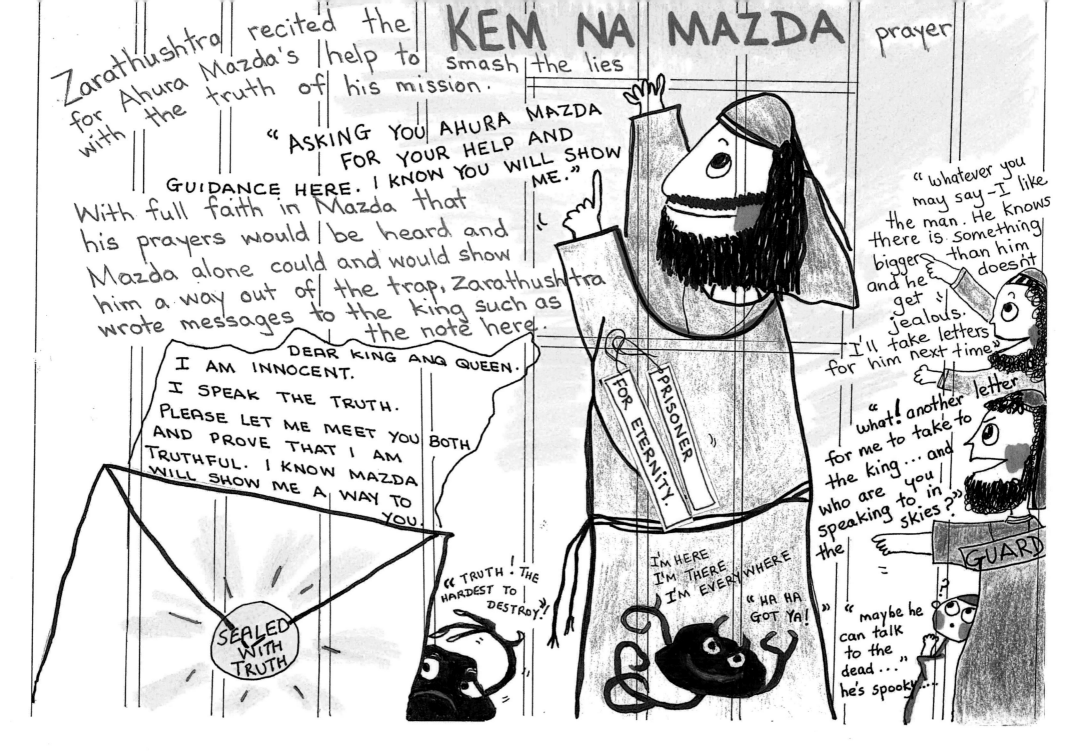

Zarathushtra when no one in teaching, travel to the was assured, his message would be heard.

knelt and prayed for guidance. He recalled, how his own land had bothered to listen to his he had prayed and was guided to court of king Vishtaspa where, he

- HAVE FAITH
  - LOTS OF FAITH
- YOU CAN CURE THE HORSE
- BELIEVE IN ME –AHURA MAZDA.

"heard a loud voice tell him, Zarathushtra, ME, AHURA MAZDA, HERE IS WHAT YOU MUST DOERS. TELL THE GUARD YOU CAN CURE THE

This time too, in a vision he BECAUSE OF YOUR FAITH IN DO TO EXPOSE THE EVIL- KING'S HORSE."

Because Zarathushtra was guided by Ahura Mazda, he knew he had nothing to worry about and calmly prayed and then gave his answer to the kind guard

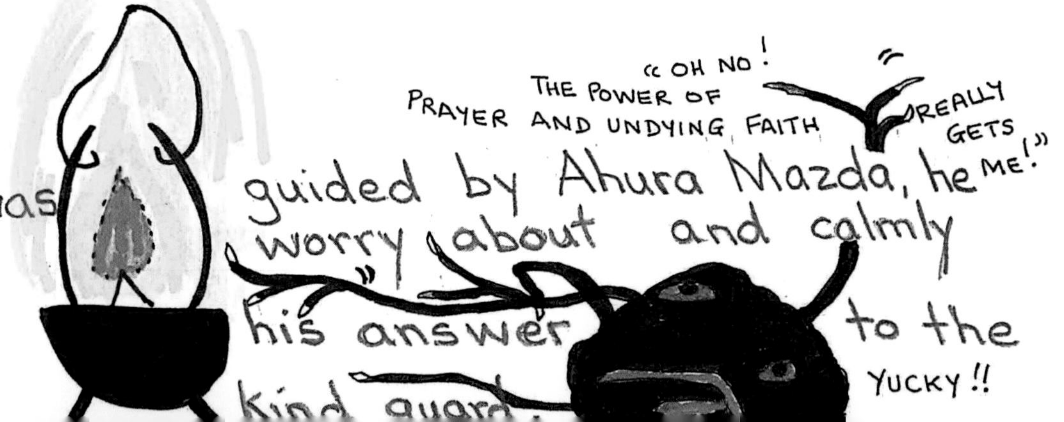

"OH NO! THE POWER OF PRAYER AND UNDYING FAITH REALLY GETS ME!"

YUCKY!!

" You are a good man, Vir and a courageous one too. stated Zarathushtra. Please tell the king that I will cure the horse. I will do it for not just my freedom but if the horse is cured, I also wish to ask that all the people of the kingdom would be asked by the king to work very hard to get rid of evil and increase goodness, in the name of AHURA MAZDA."

" Sir, are you a sort of medicine man? No vet in the land say they can cure the horse. How can you? And what if you fail Sir.... the punishment could be death

SIGH !!

" WHAT !! ME REDUNDANT NEVER....!!

...PEOPLE BEING BAD WILL NOURISH ME FOREVER (I hope)!"

Faith

"I, ZARATHUSHTRA, AM JUST A MESSENGER FOR MAZDA. I AM NO MEDICINE MAN AND I HAVE NEVER PERFORMED A MIRACLE. IT IS THROUGH MY FAITH IN MAZDA THAT I WILL CURE THE HORSE. Do please convey this last message to the king for me."

"ITS AN ORDER."

guard Zarathushtra did not have to wait long, before Vir came running back.

"URGENT" "DESPERATE"

"Zarathushtra. Here's your chance. The king calls you. Come now!! This way please. Don't lose this OPPORTUNITY."

"Thank you Vir. But first I need water to clean myself and now I need to say my prayers. Please wait."

"dear Mazda. In you I trust!"

THIS WAY, NOW!

Zarathushtra recited his prayers whilst untying and retying his kushti and concentrated fully on the power of the words.

Vir now fully understood this man's true devotion, first and foremost to God and only then to the command of the king.

However, he once more asked Zarathushtra to hurry incase the King changed his mind as all the king's advisors were so against Zarathushtra.

In strode Zarathushtra into the stable saying,
"O king Vishtaspa, all humans are born to help the creator Mazda
rid our world of suffering brought on by Ahriman.
We do this by helping those in need.

ANYTHING..." ♥

"I'll do ANYTHING FOR MY HORSE,

Here lies an animal who
like all living creatures,
lives by instinct and depends
on us humans to nurture
and protect it. (Here
Zarathushtra was indirectly
talking about the cruelty
of animal sacrifice that people
of these times were doing!)

"now lets see
our enemy
behave like
a comic!"

"thats
if he has
no powers."

"kings
already
in
mourning"

"Shall
we bet
on him?"

"dead
or
living?"

"Mazda's mission accomplished! Let's go humpy in

They are good hands."

"I dont like Humpy as my name. I only have one hump and camels from Bactria have two!! Humpy reminds me im different and I have a complex!"

"Gather together all Mazdayasnis of this land. From now on we will not just worship Mazda but make a promise to SERVE Mazda.

By doing so, our land will be a happy place in which to live. Let's try our best to Keep Ahriman from tempting us do do what is wrong and in this way We will remember what my friend Zarathushtra taught us.

(Let us call ourselves Mazdayasni Zarathushtis from now on. Followers of Zarathushtra!!)

"how I absolutely love my dad!"

"he's made us homeless."

"lets take our wickedness elsewhere. This is NO place fo us now! SIGH.

"YOU! TOO MUCH HARD WORK."

LOOT

MORE LOOT

On hearing this, the wicked no-gooders like the Sorcerers, magicians, liars and their clan slinked away never to be seen again in Vishtaspa's kingdom.

The two, now older and wiser princesses stood by the same palace gates where they had first set eyes on a strange man with light streaming from his turbaned head and questioned what he was all about.

This time, it was tears in their eyes as they watched him go!

"I thought he was a golden star. Now I wish he really was. Then I could watch my friend every night when I get lonely and sad."

"I miss him too much already!!"

Their dear friend was gone.

humans, like us dogs get too attached!!

"I will miss Zarathushtra too. He is a sort of shining star so in a way you were right Tishtrya.

But, do not be sad. Remember, he taught us to be happy and now he's gone to teach others the message.

His gift to us was enlightenment and we will keep his message alive and remember him by being happy and good."

The same man who had been disbelieved and mistrusted upon his arrival. He had now gone far away on his camel leaving behind all he came to share.

EXTENSION

And the two princesses remembered Zarathushtra daily.

MAZDA WORSHIP IN OUR KINGDOM FOR ALL

NO TO HATE

NO TO ANTI GOOD

NO TO GREED

NO TO BADNESS

"Time to go to bed now, girls." Queen Hutaosha said after they had finished, smiling at the respect with which her princesses had recited the prayer in praise of Truth and Happiness.

"You're right. We must be happy that Zarathushtra came at all. Shall we recite the ASHEM VOHU prayer? Let's chant it together."

peace already...

...beautiful!!

DEFINITE NO TO ANTI-GOD

"ha, ha that's funny. Anti-God is Ahriman isn't it... that's a definite 100%. NO NO in Mazdayasnis faith and way of life. My dad's taken a loan for my Navjote celebration soon!"

"just hearing my girl cousins pray that poem has made me feel happier. It's a magic spell. A good magic spell. I'm sure it is. I'm going to say it everyday."

Everyone in the palace had noticed how rarely the princesses quarreled or threw tantrums or told lies to escape being told off by their parents since Zarathushtra had been with them.

King Vishtaspa was overhearing the Queen's talk to their daughters and quietly praised her wisdom and all that she had learnt from Zarathushtra and he added by saying....

"ATHA JAMYAT. YATHA AFRINAMI — "SO BE IT" — IN OUR KINGDOM AND THROUGHOUT THE WORLD."

"I'm a dog. Always good.."

"It's quite easy being good if one really tries isn't it?" asked Tishtrya. when

saying goodnight to her mother and sister.

"well, sometimes Tish, I do get the urge to yell and punch you if I'm truthful, like I used to before, in the good ....err.... I mean, bad old days." princess Jehanara replied, laughing. We are only humans, you know!

"That's true". said their mother. "We do fall prey to Ahriman from time to time, like Zarathushtra explained. But he told us we must say "sorry" at once and try not to repeat our bad thoughts and bad words and bad deeds however small. In this way, little by little we CAN and WILL help Ahura Mazda to get rid of Ahriman forever."

"SIGH!!" "DOOMED!!"

AUTOGRAPH BOOK

"These prayers really work if you can pronounce the words properly.

We pray them in Avestan which was the language spoken long long ago."

I always fall asleep when she recites!!

OUR BOOK OF DAILY PRAYERS.

Also called THE **KHORDEH AVESTA**

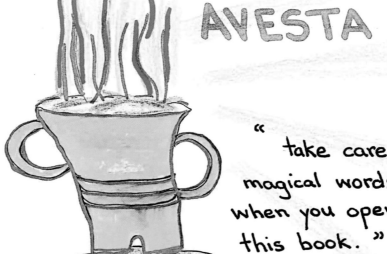

oh! I really miss my friend Zarathushtra. All he showed us is all coming back to me now.

" take care.... magical words when you open this book. "

" I cannot understand the prayers at all so they were explained to me so simply by mum."

Recite the prayers the best you can but then watch us try to really explain their meanings in the way **we** understood them."

Some very powerful words
The kushti prayers.

KEM NA MAZDA

Kem Na Mazda mavaite payum dadat , hyat ma dregvao didareshata aenanghe , anyem thwahmat athrascha manang hascha , yayao shyaothanaish ashem thraoshta . Ahura , tam moi dastvam daenayai fravao-cha.

Ke verethrem – ja thwa poi sengha yoi henti, chitra moi dam ahubish ratum chizdi ; at hoi vohu Seraosho jantu manangha, Mazda ahmai yahmai vashi kahmaichit .

Pata-no tbishyantat pairi , Mazdaoscha Armaitishcha Spentascha , nase daevi drukhsh , nase daevo- chithre, nase daevo –frakarshte, nase daevo-fradaite , apa drukhsh nase, apa drukhsh dvara, apa drukhsh vinase, apakhedhre apa- nasyehe, ma merenchainish gaethao astvaitish ashahe. Nemascha ya Armaitish izacha Ashem Vohu

ASHEM VOHU

Ashem Vohu vahishtem asti ushta asti , ushta ahmai hyat ashai vahishtai ashem.

YATHA AHU VAIRYO (AHUNA VAIRYA)

Yatha Ahu Vairyo atha ratush , ashat chit hacha, vangheush dazda manangho shyaothananam angheush Mazdai, Khshathremcha Ahurai a yim

HORMAZD KHODAE

Hormuzd Khodae , Ahreman awadashan dur awazdashtar;
Zad shekasteh bad ; Ahreman , devan, drujan,
jaduan, darvandan, kikan, karafan, sastaran ,
gunehgaran, ashmogan ,darvandan ,dushmana, frian,
zad shekasteh bad. Dush padshahan awadashan bad;
dushmana stoh bad ; dushmana awadashan bad.

Hormazd Khodae, az hama gunah patet pashemanum
az harvastin dushmat duzukht duzvarsht ,mem pa geti
Manid , oem goft , oem kard , oem jast , oem bun bud ested ,
az an gunah manashni , gavashni , kunashni, tani ravani ,
geti minoani , okhe awakhsh pasheman pa se gavashni pa
patet hom . Khshnaothra Ahurahe Mazdao; taroidite anghra-
he mainyeush . Haithyavarshtam hyat vasna fe-
rashotemem . Staomi ashem .

Ashem Vohu

Yatha Ahu Vairyo

Ashem Vohu

JASA ME AVANGHE MAZDA

Jasa me avenghe Mazda

Mazdayasno ahmi, Mazdayasno
Zarathushtrish fravarane astutascha
fravaretascha.

Astuye humatem mano, astuye hukhtem
vacho, astuye hvarshtem shyaothanem.

Astuye Daenam vanghuhim Mazdayasnim
fraspayaokhedram, nidhasnaithishem,
khaetvadatham ashaonim. Ya haitinamcha
bushyeintinamcha mazishtacha,
vahishtacha ,sraeshtacha, ya Ahuirish
Zarathushtrish.

Ahuri Mazdai vispa vohu chinahmi . Aesha
asti Daenayao Mazdayasnoish astuitish .

Ashem Vohu

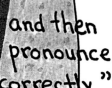

" I'm stuck in this scroll.
I think I need a prayer... any for doggies in trouble ? "

ASHEM VOHU

This is a prayer for attaining 'peace and happiness'.
Everyone wants to be happy.
The Ashem Vohu is not recited for attaining the sort of temporary happiness which comes from winning a prize, getting gifts, passing exams etc. but the kind of everlasting happiness that is the natural result of being truthful for the sake of truth, being at peace with others and in harmony with our environment.

KEM NA MAZDA.

"Who other than You, Ahura Mazda, can I turn to when I am threatened with harm? Who other than you, with your wisdom and the fire which enlightens me of the truth, will protect me and those worthy of your protection in my home?"

1

"With the blessing of your divine love and the watchfulness of your eternal spirit within me, I shall strive to recognise and reject evil which can only enter through an unguarded mind. Therefore, I seek your help to be reminded of being cautious and alert at all times."

"I'm tempted but NO, its wrong. Keep me following you Mazda."

"Go away evil!" NOW!! IT'S AN ORDER!!"

SISTERS JEWELS AND SECRET DIARY

YOU CAN BE PRINCESS No. 1 SOON.

TOGETHER WE CAN GET RID OF YOUR BOSSY OLDER SIS.

"I'm using all my evil strength to coax her. Her mind seems too powerful to lure her from goodness. DRAT !!"

AHUNA VAIRYA (YATHA AHU VAIRYO)

This is a prayer for 'action'. Ahura Mazda has provided us all with a good mind and a sound body and has put in us good energy with which to perform good actions so as to help good win and evil lose.

It is by reciting this prayer that we gain the necessary strength to seek out and help whosoever and whatever good cause needs helpers.

AHURA MAZDA KHODAE

There are unseen enemies all around me — wicked persons and also wicked thoughts. These confront me in my daily life.
I first need to recognise them and then keep my distance from wrong minded persons as well as those thoughts which I know are NOT good for me.

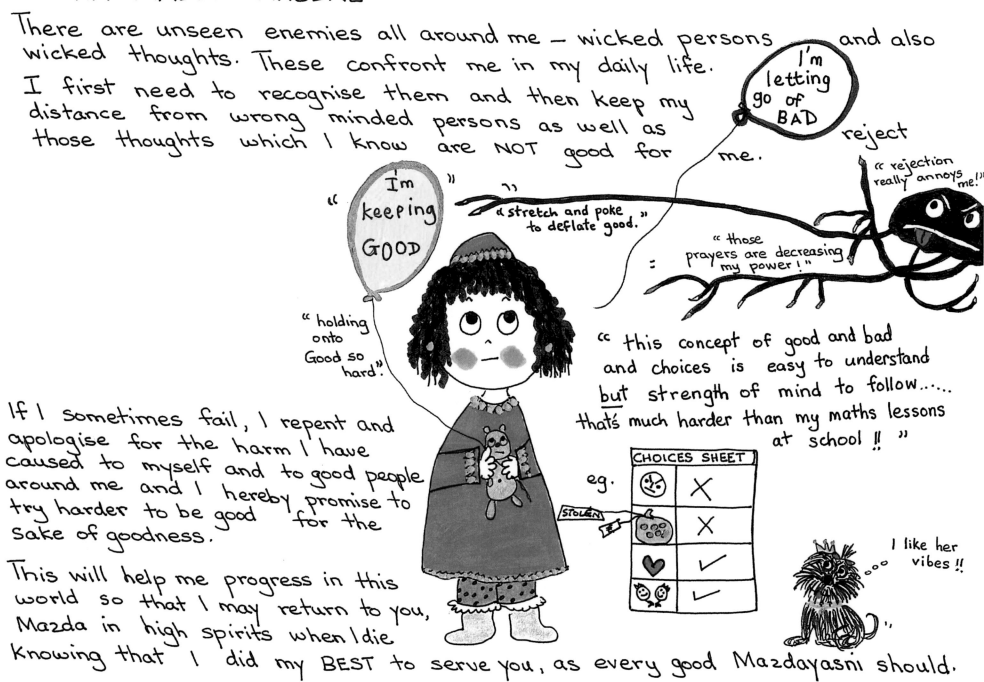

"I'm letting go of BAD"

reject

"rejection really annoys me!"

"I'm keeping GOOD"

"stretch and poke to deflate good."

"those prayers are decreasing my power!"

"holding onto Good so hard".

"this concept of good and bad and choices is easy to understand but strength of mind to follow...... that's much harder than my maths lessons at school !!"

If I sometimes fail, I repent and apologise for the harm I have caused to myself and to good people around me and I hereby promise to try harder to be good for the sake of goodness.

eg.

CHOICES SHEET

☹	X
STOLEN 🎃	X
♥	✓
👫	✓

I like her vibes !!

This will help me progress in this world so that I may return to you, Mazda in high spirits when I die knowing that I did my BEST to serve you, as every good Mazdayasni should.

DOING MY KUSHTI WHILE SAYING AHURA MAZDA KHODAE

" When the first knot is tied, the devotee should remember that the firmament above and the earth below, though they seem seperate to the eyes of man, are yet bounded together as one whole.

The second knot should remind him that Holy Zarathushtra was the Prophet of Ahura Mazda.

The third knot should remind him that what is revealed in our religion is pure and sublime and that we have to accept the teachings faithfully.

The fourth knot should remind the devotee that he is bound to serve humanity and to be a co-sharer in the joys and sorrows of his fellow man. "

" Tishtrya, I watched Zarathushtra instruct papa with knot tying of the kushti so I will explain please!! "

HEY,
" you've learnt the above by heart word for word sister !! It's the exact quote for tying the four knots made while the kushti is tied and the quote is by Framroz Rustomjee from his book ' Daily Prayers of the Zoroastrians'.
Good memory, sister dear !! "

they are powerful with their head full of magical words ..

" I hate these two know-it-all's. Would love to strangle them but

PRAYERS

JASA ME AVANGHE MAZDA

This is a solemn declaration of an individual's formal entry into the Mazda-worshipping faith. In this prayer, that person seeks the help of Ahura Mazda, to remain true to the teachings of the Mazdayasni faith, as explained by the prophet Zarathushtra.

The devotee also pledges obedience to the important rule of practising good thoughts, good words and good deeds and promises to cherish the religious beliefs and customs of the faith as being the best for him/her.

" ... and I will be faithful to Mazda and always try my best to remember GOOD thoughts GOOD words and GOOD deeds! "

'HUMATA HUKHTA HUVARASHTA'

" It's a huge huge promise I have to make and I fully understand what I am taking on and I WANT to !! "

" can you believe it; only 3 more sleep get-ups till its our Navjote, princess Tishtrya !! No more just dreaming Navjotes like we've been imagining ! "

KUSHTI PRAYERS

" it's my walkies time !! they also made that promise that I'd be walked... so c'mon girls." (only take on what you can chew!)

WOOF!!

LIGHT VERSUS DARKNESS

ITS ALL IN YOUR HANDS EVERY SINGLE DAY!

HELPFUL • CHEERFUL • KIND • GOOD • HARD WORKING • SINCERE • TRUTHFUL • HONEST

LETS PLAY A GAME. YOU NEED 2 BALLOONS

The lighter coloured balloon represents MAZDA and light and the darker one, all that is dark and bad.

"THE BIGGER..." "THE BETTER"

colours — yellow and black

• As you blow up your light coloured balloon, let each blow, be good thoughts of all the good things you have done. (tie up your filled up balloon of goodness.)

"I've chosen my two

• As you blow up your darker balloon, remember any bad thoughts or actions you have done !!

"We all make mistakes!"

Now release the air out of this dark balloon and try to keep this balloon shrivelled up, apologising as you make this balloon flatter and flatter and smaller always than your lighter balloon of goodness.

"oh! how I love being incharge of myself. Its me who controls me !!" Fw

daily goodness and badness to be who I want to be !!"

"its all in my hands too...." "see this PINK...."

"balloon of goodness. YUK..."

ITS ALL in my hands.

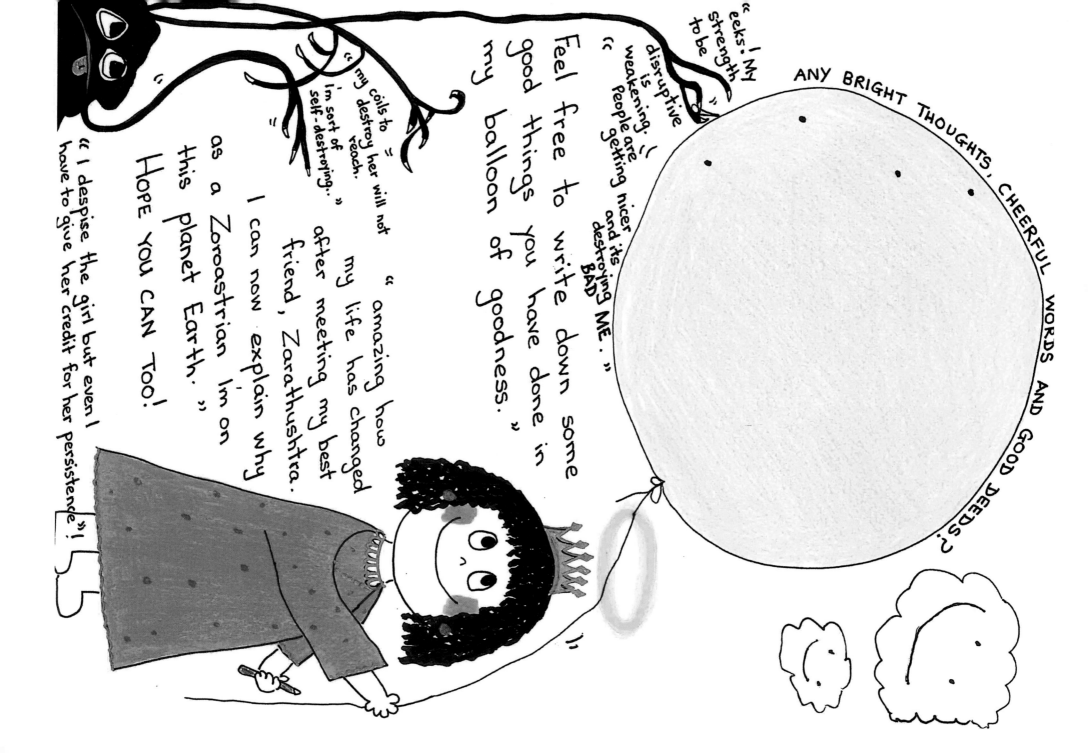

Now feel free to write down some
bad thoughts or things you've said or done.
(maybe some days your balloon may remain
empty — you will then be a winner and
feel so good !.)

"hey Tishtrya.
You know I am kind of Perfect.
So how am I landed holding onto
everyone's bad stuff ?? "

"FRESHLY
STOLEN"

"KINGS
JEWELS"

"BADNESS be the new you! we could"
could be princess friends!".

ANY DARK THOUGHTS, BAD WORDS
AND NASTY DEEDS?

RUB THEM OFF AT
THE END OF A FRESH
AND START ON A
SLATE BALLOON

"c'mon guys!
fill her up."
get tempted.

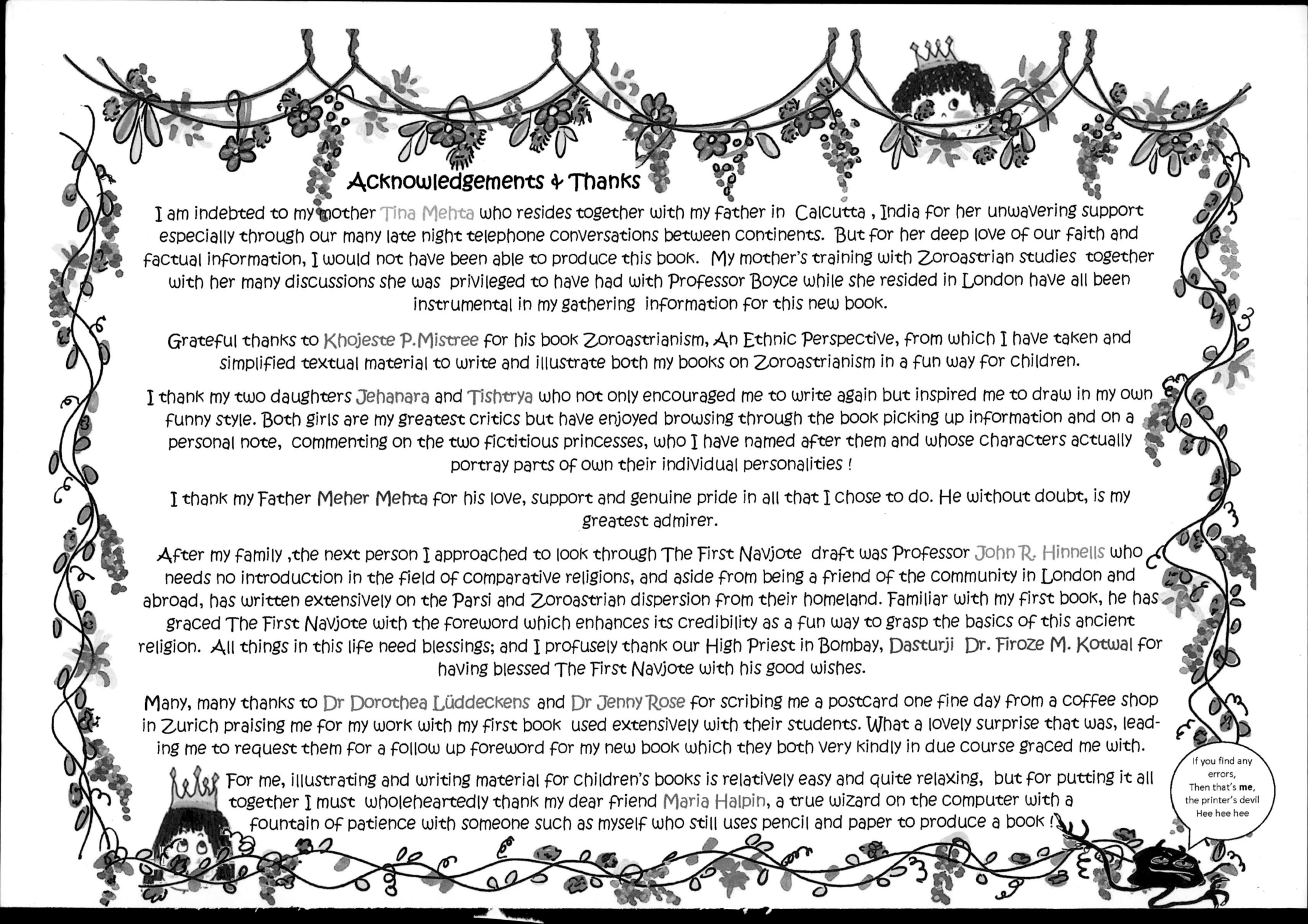

Acknowledgements & Thanks

I am indebted to my mother Tina Mehta who resides together with my father in Calcutta, India for her unwavering support especially through our many late night telephone conversations between continents. But for her deep love of our faith and factual information, I would not have been able to produce this book. My mother's training with Zoroastrian studies together with her many discussions she was privileged to have had with Professor Boyce while she resided in London have all been instrumental in my gathering information for this new book.

Grateful thanks to Khojeste P. Mistree for his book Zoroastrianism, An Ethnic Perspective, from which I have taken and simplified textual material to write and illustrate both my books on Zoroastrianism in a fun way for children.

I thank my two daughters Jehanara and Tishtrya who not only encouraged me to write again but inspired me to draw in my own funny style. Both girls are my greatest critics but have enjoyed browsing through the book picking up information and on a personal note, commenting on the two fictitious princesses, who I have named after them and whose characters actually portray parts of own their individual personalities!

I thank my Father Meher Mehta for his love, support and genuine pride in all that I chose to do. He without doubt, is my greatest admirer.

After my family, the next person I approached to look through The First Navjote draft was Professor John R. Hinnells who needs no introduction in the field of comparative religions, and aside from being a friend of the community in London and abroad, has written extensively on the Parsi and Zoroastrian dispersion from their homeland. Familiar with my first book, he has graced The First Navjote with the foreword which enhances its credibility as a fun way to grasp the basics of this ancient religion. All things in this life need blessings; and I profusely thank our High Priest in Bombay, Dasturji Dr. Firoze M. Kotwal for having blessed The First Navjote with his good wishes.

Many, many thanks to Dr Dorothea Lüddeckens and Dr Jenny Rose for scribing me a postcard one fine day from a coffee shop in Zurich praising me for my work with my first book used extensively with their students. What a lovely surprise that was, leading me to request them for a follow up foreword for my new book which they both very kindly in due course graced me with.

For me, illustrating and writing material for children's books is relatively easy and quite relaxing, but for putting it all together I must wholeheartedly thank my dear friend Maria Halpin, a true wizard on the computer with a fountain of patience with someone such as myself who still uses pencil and paper to produce a book!

If you find any errors,
Then that's me,
the printer's devil
Hee hee hee